L M JONES

Nest Egg Necessities

Basic financial considerations for growing families

Contents

1   Introduction   1

2   Assessing Your Financial Health   5

3   Budgeting for Baby   14

4   Insurance and Healthcare   21

5   The Cost and Benefits of Parental Leave   28

6   Saving For Your Child's Future   34

7   Estate Planning and Wills   42

8   Conclusions   49

9   Resources   52

1

Introduction

Having a child is a life-changing event. As you embark on this exciting journey, you must recognize the importance of proper financial planning. Ensuring a stable and secure future for your child and your family as a whole can help reduce the amount of stress and uncertainty in your life. This book aims to give you a solid starting point for planning your financial future and to suggest a few things you may have yet to consider that could benefit you and your child no matter what the future holds. This book does NOT give specific investment advice, nor is it to be used in place of a qualified financial advisor.

Why is financial planning important, especially if you are expecting? It can help you:

- **Build a Strong Foundation**: Financial planning helps lay the foundation for a financially secure future. A strong foundation can help limit stress due to unexpected expenses or thinking of money for the future.
-

- **Manage Expenses**: Kids are expensive. Between medical costs, childcare, education, and daily necessities, the cost of raising a child from birth to 18 in the US was estimated to be over $300,000 in 2022. A solid financial plan will help you anticipate, prioritize and manage these expenses more efficiently. A plan allows you to track your spending, create a budget, find savings and make informed decisions to ensure your money is utilized effectively.

-

- **Minimize Financial Stress**: Financial stress can affect your mental and physical health and impact your ability to provide for your child's needs. Engaging in financial planning can help you alleviate anxiety and stress related to your finances. As a new parent, you will have enough on your plate, so knowing that you have a comprehensive strategy to handle any financial challenges can help you focus on the truly important thing: your child.

-

- **Secure Your Child's Future**: Everyone wants their child to have a bright future. Planning for that bright future means considering education, healthcare, and inheritance. By starting your planning early, you can save for their education, ensure adequate healthcare coverage, and establish a robust financial safety net. If you have not already, start now. A solid financial plan, no matter when it began, can help provide the most monetary assistance for your child's future.

-

- **Maximize Opportunities**: Financial planning allows you to identify and seize previously unaware opportunities. Planning can benefit your family in the long run. By carefully managing your finances and consulting a professional, you can explore investments, optimize tax strategies, and leverage financial tools to enhance your financial situation, which can help provide a better future for your family.

The purpose of this book is to serve as a basic guide for individuals or couples looking to start a family. While not comprehensive, it aims to empower you with knowledge and tools to know which questions to ask and some currently popular options. Additionally, this book contends that while a college savings account is a good start, other things must be considered to help secure your family's financial future.

In this book, we will discuss the following:

- **Assessing Your Financial Health**: How to understand your financial situation clearly.
- **Budgeting for Baby**: How to plan for the costs associated with having a baby and help guide you in creating a baby-specific budget.
- **Insurance and Healthcare**: What is their role in your growing family's finances, and what are some options to consider.
- **Parental Leave**: Balancing work and family life can be challenging during the transition to parenthood.
- **Saving for Your Child's Future**: Planning for your child's education and long-term financial stability.
- **Estate Planning and Wills**: Securing your child's future extends beyond a bank account.

By recognizing the importance of financial preparedness and engaging in planning and open communication, you can provide a stable and secure environment for your growing family.

2

Assessing Your Financial Health

You may be asking yourself how to get started. You may feel overwhelmed by the whole idea of financial planning, especially with everything else that is going on in your life. That is normal. Take a deep breath and start at the beginning.

The first step is understanding your financial starting point. This is true whether you are starting a family, a business, or just trying to save money for a rainy day. Regardless of the reason, it is crucial to understand your current financial status to maximize your finances. Understanding your income, expenses, and debt and identifying areas for improvement are essential steps toward responsible financial planning for your growing family.

2.1 The Importance of Assessing Your Financial Health

Assessing your financial health is like taking a snapshot of your current financial situation. Looking at this snapshot can be comforting, intimidating or down-right scary, but it is a necessary evil. You can't fix what you don't know is broken, and no matter how hard we wish, ignoring it will not make it go away. Usually, the longer you ignore a money problem, the bigger the problem grows. By evaluating your overall financial well-being, you can rip off the metaphorical band-aid, identify any areas that require attention or improvement, and correct them. By conducting a thorough and honest assessment, you will gain valuable insights that can be translated into actions to maintain or improve your financial standing. Consider this practice for being a new parent: take a deep breath and jump in!

Five benefits of understanding your financial health:

1. You can identify and rectify any financial mistakes or inefficiencies.
2. You can measure your progress towards your financial goals.
3. You can make informed decisions regarding savings, investments, and expenses.
4. It provides you with a foundation for developing a comprehensive financial plan.
5. It helps you anticipate and prepare for economic challenges or unexpected events.

2.2 Assessing Your Income

Income is an essential part of your financial health. Evaluating your income involves understanding where your income comes from, how reliable that source is, and if there is potential for growth. Here are four key steps to assess your income:

1.<u>Identify all sources of income</u>: List your income streams, including salary, bonuses, rental income, dividends, and any other sources (odd jobs, freelancing, annuities, etc).

2.<u>Evaluate income stability</u>: Consider the reliability and consistency of your income sources. Assess whether they are subject to fluctuations and whether those fluctuations are predictable. Having a child definitely counts as a future fluctuation.

3.<u>Determine growth potential</u>: Determine if there are opportunities to increase your income. This includes promotions, changing jobs, or acquiring additional skills. Ask yourself if there is a time frame in which you could expect to receive or negotiate a promotion or raise. Do you get bonuses for meeting company goals? Do you get stock options for your company? Could your side hustle be expanded? Could you increase your margins without losing customers? All of those can factor into your future income.

4.<u>Calculate your net income</u>: Calculate your monthly average net income by deducting taxes and other deductions (such as insurance costs, social security, etc) from your gross income (total amount of money you make). For most, this is done for you by your employer before your pay is put in your bank account. If you are self-employed, this would be the amount after pre-tax deductions and taxes. Check your pay slip for the breakdown, so you know where your money is going.

By assessing your income, you will clearly understand your current income and earning potential. This will enable you to make informed decisions regarding financial goals for you and your growing family.

2.3 Analyzing Your Expenses

Now let's discuss one of people's least favorite money topics – expenses. Expenses are the money that leaves your bank account every month to pay for things you need or want. Analyzing your expenses involves examining your spending patterns, differentiating between essential and discretionary expenses, and identifying areas where you can reduce costs. Follow these five steps to assess your expenses effectively:

1.<u>Categorize your expenses</u>: Group your expenses into categories such as housing, utilities, transportation, groceries, entertainment, debt payments, and savings. This will help you see the breakdown of where your money is going every month.

2.<u>Differentiate between essential and non-essential expenses</u>: Identify expenses that are necessary for your basic needs (e.g., food, shelter, utilities) and those that are discretionary (e.g., entertainment, dining out, new clothes, etc).

3.<u>Track your expenses</u>: Sometimes, looking at just one month may over or under-estimate your expenses. This can occur if a month has holidays like Christmas, birthdays or summer versus school months. Instead, maintain a record of your expenses for a more extended period, such as three months, to understand your spending patterns accurately. This may mean you need to average your spending between the months to understand better what you typically spend in a month.

4.<u>Evaluate your spending habits</u>: Take a look at your spending patterns and find areas where you can scale back or adjust to align with your financial goals. Once you know where your money is going, you can look at that category and see if any savings can be found. Check your credit card statement for recurrent expenses and think if they are necessary or could be reduced. Do you watch that streaming service often enough to make it worth it? Could you reduce the number of times a month you dine out? Have you forgotten to cancel a monthly membership? Can you call and negotiate your monthly cable or phone bill? These are a few examples of common places to cut spending.

5.<u>Create a budget</u>: Based on your spending analysis, develop a realistic budget (this will differ from person to person and may require some compromise with your partner) that allocates your income to various expense categories. These categories can include baby-specific savings. A more specific baby budget will be discussed in Chapter 3.

By assessing your expenses, you gain control over your financial life, identify potential areas for improvement, and ensure that your spending aligns with your long-term financial objectives. Each of these will change throughout your pregnancy, your child's life, and your life. Be sure to revisit and reassess as needed, with an annual check recommended.

2.4 Assessing Your Debt

Debt can significantly impact your financial health, so evaluating your debt situation is important. Debt is often the aspect of one's financial situation that makes people feel defeated. Knowledge and having a plan to erase that debt will help you overcome that feeling. Assessing your debt involves understanding the types of debt you have, the interest rates, the repayment terms, and the impact of debt on your overall financial well-being. Consider the following steps when evaluating your debt:

1.<u>Identify your debts</u>: Make a comprehensive list of all your debts, including credit card debt, student loans, mortgages, car loans, and any other outstanding obligations.

2.<u>Review interest rates</u>: Interest rates can cause your debt to skyrocket even if you pay monthly. Know the rates for each of your debts and how often that interest is compounded. Look into ways to lower that interest rate, such as refinancing.

3.<u>Examine repayment terms</u>: Understand the repayment terms for each debt, including the monthly payment amounts and the length of the repayment period. Know how much of the monthly payment goes toward principal versus interest if you are repaying a loan. Look into if it is possible to change those terms to benefit you and your monthly income.

4.<u>Calculate debt-to-income ratio</u>: Calculate your debt-to-income ratio by dividing your total monthly debt payments by your monthly gross income. This ratio helps determine your ability to manage debt.

5.<u>Develop a debt repayment strategy</u>: Based on your assessment, create a plan to pay off your debts systematically. Consider strategies such as the snowball method (paying off debts from smallest to most significant) or the avalanche method (paying off debts with the highest interest rates first). Choose one that works best for your personality and one that you will stick with.

Assessing your debt empowers you to take control of your financial future, develop effective debt repayment strategies, and work towards achieving financial security for your family.

2.5 Identifying Areas for Improvement

Once you have assessed your income, expenses, and debt, it is essential to identify areas for improvement. Here are some common areas where individuals often find room for enhancement:

- <u>Increasing income</u>: Explore opportunities to boost your income, such as negotiating a raise, starting a side business, or investing in professional development.

- <u>Reducing expenses and/or downsizing</u>: Look for ways to reduce non-essential expenses, negotiate better deals on essential expenses, or find more cost-effective alternatives. Also, figure out if there are any large-ticket items you could sell or downsize, such as cars, boats, storage units, furniture, expensive equipment, etc. This only applies to items you do not need. You can take the proceeds from those sales and put them toward debt payments or savings.

- <u>Eliminating high-interest debt</u>: Large debts with high interest, such as credit cards, will grow faster than small debts. Eliminating those debts will reduce the amount of interest you pay over time. However, if paying off debts from smallest to largest fits your personality more, do that even if you are not paying off the high-interest debt first.

- <u>Building an emergency fund</u>: Establish an emergency fund to cover unexpected expenses and protect yourself from financial hardships. Aim for a $1000 emergency fund.

- <u>Investing and saving for the future</u>: Start saving for retirement and other long-term goals by investing in retirement accounts, such as 401(k)s or IRAs, or exploring other investment options. Options for educational savings accounts will be discussed in chapter 6.

Identifying areas for improvement allows you to develop a road map for enhancing your financial health and achieving your financial goals. With a new baby on the way, setting goals and leaving yourself some wiggle room is crucial. A child will always come with unexpected expenses – having a financial cushion will go a long way in preventing future stress.

Assessing your financial health is vital to achieving financial stability and success. By evaluating your income, expenses, and debt, you gain valuable insights into your current financial situation and identify areas for improvement. With this knowledge, you can make informed decisions, develop a comprehensive financial plan, and work towards achieving your financial goals and maintaining financial security for your growing family. Remember, assessing your financial health is an ongoing process that requires regular review and adjustment as your circumstances change.

3

Budgeting for Baby

As you prepare to welcome a new addition to your family, it is essential to understand and plan for the financial responsibilities that come with having a baby. Budgeting allows you a basic plan to help anticipate and manage the costs associated with the baby's arrival, ensuring a smoother transition into parenthood. This chapter will guide you through estimating the expenses, creating a baby-specific budget, and providing tips on cutting expenses and saving money along the way.

3.1 Estimating the Costs Associated with Having a Baby:

There are many expenses that come with growing your family. Some are obvious while others may be easier to overlook.Below are some of the most common expenses to consider and work into your family's budget when as you plan for your baby.

- <u>Medical Expenses</u>: The first step in estimating the costs of having a baby involves understanding the medical expenses associated with pre-natal care, childbirth, and post-natal care. These may include doctor visits, ultrasound scans, blood tests, delivery charges, hospital stays, and necessary medications. Research and consult with your healthcare provider or insurance company to clearly understand these expenses. Many medical facilities and/or states offer a self-service estimate tool online as more laws requiring price transparency are passed.

- <u>Baby Gear and Essentials</u>: Babies require various essentials, including diapers, clothing, feeding supplies, a crib or bassinet, strollers, car seats, and other necessary baby gear. Research the average costs of these items and consider whether you'll be purchasing new or second-hand items—additionally, factor in ongoing expenses for items such as diapers, formula, clothing and baby food.

- <u>Childcare</u>: Childcare costs can be significant, especially if both parents plan to continue working full-time and you have no family in your immediate area. Look into the options available in your area, such as daycare centers, nannies, or in-home care, and obtain estimates for their monthly or weekly costs. Remember that these costs may vary depending on location and the specific services offered.

- <u>Healthcare and Insurance</u>: Assess the impact on your health insurance coverage and determine any additional costs associated with adding your child to your plan. Understand the co-payments, deductibles, and coverage limits for pediatric visits, vaccinations, and other medical needs. If necessary, explore the option of purchasing additional insurance coverage for your child's healthcare expenses.

- <u>Parental Leave</u>: Consider the financial implications of taking parental leave from work. Be aware of your rights, your company's policy regarding paid or unpaid leave, and any short-term disability benefits that may apply. Factor in any potential loss of income during this period and plan your finances accordingly.

3.2 Creating a Baby-Specific Budget:

Now that you have an outline of the most likely expenses, it is time to make a baby budget. This will help you determine how much money would make have you prepared for your new addition as well as show you how you may need to adjust any existing spending to prepare for the increased cost of a child. Here are five key points to creating your new budget to serve your family:

1.<u>Evaluate Your Current Financial Situation</u>: Before creating a baby-specific budget, assess your financial health as described in the previous chapter. Understand your monthly cash flow and identify areas where you can reduce expenses or reallocate funds to accommodate the additional costs associated with having a baby.

2.Identify Essential Baby Categories: Create budget categories tailored to your baby's needs. This may include categories such as medical expenses from pregnancy, pediatrician costs, essential baby gear, non-essential baby gear, single purchase (i.e., stroller) vs. repeat purchase (i.e., diapers), baby items, childcare, education fund and health insurance.

3.Allocate Funds: Determine how much you need to allocate to each category based on your estimates of associated costs. Be realistic and consider any potential fluctuations in expenses. Always overestimate your associated costs. This ensures you have the funds you need or some extra left over if you find unexpected savings.

4.Prioritize Savings: Including a savings category in your baby-specific budget is important. This allows you to set aside money for future expenses, emergencies, and long-term goals, such as your child's education. Start saving as early as possible, even if it's a small amount, as it can accumulate over time.

5.Regularly Review and Adjust: Your baby-specific budget should be a dynamic document that evolves as you move through your pregnancy and as your baby grows. Review your budget regularly to ensure it accurately reflects your actual expenses. Make adjustments as necessary to align with your changing needs and financial goals.

3.3 Tips for Cutting Expenses and Saving Money:

Anytime you are budgeting for new expenses, especially large new expenses, it is always a good idea to look at ways to cut costs. This is especially true if there may be unexpected costs that pop up, which is very common with a new child. You probably won't think of every cost so having extra money is never a bad thing. Look to cut costs and save by doing any or all of the following (please note this is not an exhaustive list and you may come up with other ways to mitigate any new expenses):

- Comparison Shopping: When purchasing baby gear and essentials, compare prices from different retailers and consider buying second-hand items in good condition from kid-specific resale shops/online sites (Kid-to-Kid, Once Upon a Child, etc.) or local online marketplaces (Facebook marketplace, craigslist, etc.). Look for deals, discounts, and sales to save money on necessary purchases.

- Hand-me-downs: Look to your friends and family. If any recently had children, they may be willing to give or loan you items their child has outgrown. Please remember they are also allowed NOT to give or lend you items.

- Prioritize Essential Items: Focus on purchasing essential items first, such as a safe crib or bassinet, car seat, and clothing. Remember, babies grow quickly, so clothes may only fit for a short period, so mainly getting gently used or hand-me-down garments with a few brand-new outfits may be more financially savvy. Also, a more expensive piece of baby gear with multiple functions and/or grows with your child, such as a stroller that is also a car seat and folds down to a bassinet, may be a more economical choice than three separate items. Avoid unnecessary or extravagant purchases that may strain your budget until all your essential purchases are covered.

- Baby Shower and Gift Registry: Consider having a baby shower or creating a gift registry to receive needed baby items as gifts from family and friends. This can help alleviate some of the financial burden of purchasing baby essentials. This does NOT mean you will receive everything on your list, so do not use this as your only way of getting essential gear.

- Breastfeeding and Homemade Baby Food: This area is only effective if doing these does NOT place additional strain on the parents. Breastfeeding your baby will help you save on the cost of formula. Additionally, you can prepare homemade baby food instead of purchasing pre-packaged options to reduce expenses. If neither are viable options, formula and pre-packaged baby food are absolutely fine and should not be a source of stress or guilt.

- <u>Evaluate Childcare Options</u>: Explore different childcare options and compare their costs. Consider alternatives, such as sharing childcare responsibilities with a trusted family member or friend, to reduce expenses. Determine if remote work is possible or could be paired with only a few days a week in the office to minimize childcare requirements.

- <u>Examine typical cost-cutting efforts</u>: Reduce utility bills by implementing energy-saving measures in your home – use energy-efficient appliances, adjust thermostat settings, and be mindful of water and electricity consumption. Reevaluate subscriptions and memberships - cancel or pause those that are seldom or never used and are not essential. You can redirect any savings to your baby budget or emergency fund.

Budgeting for your baby is crucial to financial planning before starting a family. By estimating the costs associated with having a baby, creating a baby-specific budget, and implementing strategies to cut expenses and save money, you can ensure a financially stable future for your growing family. Regularly review and adjust your budget to accommodate changing needs and priorities. With careful planning and mindful spending, you can confidently navigate parenthood's financial challenges and provide the best possible start for your child.

4

Insurance and Healthcare

When starting a family, it is essential to understand the intricacies of insurance and healthcare. This chapter will discuss some basics about pregnancy and childbirth insurance, other insurance needs such as life insurance and disability insurance, and planning for healthcare expenses. This includes looking into the benefits of setting up a Health Savings Account (HSA) to manage healthcare costs effectively. Please note that the insurance and healthcare information is based on those in the United States. If you are from outside the US, you will need to research how this may apply and the options available in your home country.

4.1 Health Insurance Coverage for Pregnancy and Childbirth:
Understanding Your Health Insurance Policy: The first step in navigating health insurance coverage for pregnancy and childbirth is thoroughly reviewing your health insurance policy. Look for information on maternity care, prenatal visits, childbirth, post-natal care, and any associated costs. Pay attention to coverage limitations, deductibles, co-payments, and network

restrictions. Call your insurance company and ask questions to understand your policy better.

- Employer-Sponsored Health Insurance: If you have employer-sponsored health insurance, review the benefits package provided by your employer. Understand what services are covered, potential out-of-pocket expenses, what happens in case of an emergency, whether there are any waiting periods for maternity coverage, and whether you need to make any changes or additions to your policy to accommodate your pregnancy and your baby once the child is born. Adding a dependent to your policy may increase your health insurance rates. Discuss that with your provider directly or go through your HR department to know the process and costs.

- Individual Health Insurance: If you have individual health insurance, review your policy and contact your insurance provider for information regarding maternity coverage. Understand the specific services covered, potential out-of-pocket expenses, what happens in case of an emergency, and any waiting periods that may apply. Adding a dependent to your policy may increase your health insurance rates, so be sure to ask about this process once the baby has been born.

- State-Sponsored Health Insurance Programs: Some states

offer health insurance programs specifically designed for low-income individuals or families. Research whether your state has any programs that provide coverage for pregnancy, childbirth or young children and if you would qualify. Examples include Medicaid and the Children's Health Insurance Program (CHIP).

Contact your insurance provider directly if you are unsure about your coverage or have specific questions. Their customer service representatives should be able to provide detailed information about your policy, coverage options, and any additional benefits available to you.

4.2. Exploring Other Insurance Needs:

Although health insurance is the first type that comes to mind, it is not the only form of insurance that it may be beneficial to explore.Look into other types of insurance and see if they could be of use now that your family is growing. This may include:

Life Insurance: Life insurance is an important consideration when starting a family. It provides financial protection for your loved ones in the event of your death. Assess your life insurance needs based on factors such as your income, debt, future expenses (such as childcare and education), and the financial well-being of your family. Consult with insurance professionals to determine the appropriate coverage amount and policy type. Life insurance is not necessary; however, it could be beneficial in a worst-case scenario. It can always be canceled later.

<u>Disability Insurance</u>: Disability insurance is designed to provide income replacement if you become unable to work due to a disability or illness. Evaluate your employer's disability insurance coverage, if available, and consider supplementing it with additional individual coverage if needed. Review the policy terms, waiting periods, and benefit amounts to ensure adequate protection for your family's financial stability. Disability insurance is not required but could prove beneficial in the case of an accident. It can always be canceled later.

<u>Homeowners or Renters Insurance</u>: As you prepare for your baby's arrival, it is essential to review your homeowner's or renter's insurance policy. Ensure that your policy covers the value of your belongings, including any new baby-related items. Consider adding additional coverage for valuable items or liability protection to safeguard your family's financial security.

<u>Auto Insurance</u>: Review your auto insurance policy and consider increasing your coverage limits to provide additional protection for your family. Once your child is old enough to drive (it will be sooner than you think), look into other discounts such as multi-car, good student and away-from-home student discounts.

You may decide that none of these are worth acquiring or modifying your existing policies now and that is perfectly fine. However, it is always good to know your options and make that determination using all available information.

4.3 A HSA may be worth looking into:

If you qualify, a Health Savings Account (HSA) may be a direction for you to go. A HSA is a tax-advantaged savings account that allows you to save money for healthcare expenses. It offers several benefits, including tax deductions on contributions, tax-free growth, and tax-free withdrawals for eligible healthcare expenses. Research HSAs and determine if you are eligible to open one. These funds could be used for some of your prenatal and post-natal health expenses. Consult with a financial advisor to understand the contribution limits, investment options, and withdrawal rules associated with an HSA.

- Estimating Healthcare Expenses: When planning for healthcare expenses, it is essential to consider both expected and unexpected costs. Estimate the expenses associated with prenatal care, delivery, post-natal care, and vaccinations. Additionally, you should factor in ongoing healthcare costs for your child, including well-child visits and immunizations.

- Setting Up an HSA: If eligible and financially able, consider setting up an HSA before the arrival of your baby. Research different HSA providers, compare fees and features, and choose a provider that aligns with your needs. Understand the process of contributing to your HSA, including payroll deductions or personal contributions, and educate yourself on eligible healthcare expenses that can be paid using HSA funds.

- <u>Maximizing HSA Contributions</u>: Aim to contribute the maximum allowable amount to your HSA each year. This will help you build a substantial reserve of funds to cover current and future healthcare expenses for you during your pregnancy as well as after for your family. Automate your contributions whenever possible to ensure consistent savings. Keep in mind that an early withdrawal of money for non-medical purposes may be subject to higher taxes and penalties. However, HSA money you don't use during your pregnancy can be used in the future. This makes it an attractive way to have some money saved in case of a medical emergency.

- <u>Tracking and Managing HSA Expenses</u>: Keep detailed records of healthcare expenses paid for using your HSA funds. Retain receipts and statements to substantiate withdrawals made from your HSA. This will facilitate accurate record-keeping and simplify the process of tax reporting.

Understanding insurance coverage for pregnancy and childbirth, exploring other insurance needs, and planning for healthcare expenses are crucial steps in ensuring the financial security of your growing family. Review your health insurance policy, contact your insurance provider for clarification, and explore additional options such as life and disability insurance. Estimate healthcare expenses, consider setting up a Health Savings

Account (HSA) to manage healthcare costs effectively, and if you do utilize a HAS, maximize your contributions to secure the financial well-being of your family. With proper planning and informed decision-making, you can navigate the complexities of insurance and healthcare, providing peace of mind as you embark on the journey of parenthood.

5

The Cost and Benefits of Parental Leave

The transition to parenthood often brings the need for maternity and paternity leave. Taking time off work to care for your newborn is a significant decision that requires careful financial planning. This chapter will focus on some basic steps for planning for your familial leave. Again, this information is specific to the United States. If you are from outside the US, you will need to investigate any similar practices and the laws of your country.

5.1 Determining Your Rights and Benefits Regarding Parental Leave:

When it comes to parental leave, it varies from person to person. Knowing what you are entitled to as a new parent can help you plan better for how much time you will be away from work, how that will impact your income, and provide some peace of mind should an emergency arise. To use your parental leave most efficiently it is best to:

<u>Know Your Legal Rights</u>: Familiarize yourself with the laws and regulations governing parental leave in your country or region. Research the entitlements, duration, and eligibility criteria for maternity and paternity leave. Understand any specific rights and any possible additional benefits.

<u>Employer Policies and Benefits</u>: Review your employer's policies regarding maternity and paternity leave. Some companies may offer more generous leave policies than legally required. Understand the duration of leave, whether paid or unpaid and any specific conditions or documentation required. Also, look into your current bank of paid time off and sick days to see if there may be wiggle room for using some of those for leave and if your employer allows you to use them instead of unpaid leave.

<u>Family and Medical Leave Act (FMLA) in the United States</u>: If you are employed in the United States, understand the qualifications for and the provisions of the Family and Medical Leave Act (FMLA). FMLA provides eligible employees with up to 12 weeks of unpaid leave for the birth or adoption of a child while protecting their job position. Some of the FMLA unpaid leave can also be utilized for pregnancy complications.

<u>Communicate with Human Resources</u>: Engage in open communication with your employer's Human Resources department. Seek clarification on your entitlements, benefits, and any necessary procedures for applying for parental leave. Obtain the required forms and understand the notification requirements to ensure a smooth transition.

All of these can help you determine how you want to approach your time with your newborn. Make sure to get any plan or agreement between you and your employer in writing or email format to reference later. This could save you a headache down the road.

5.2 Planning Financially for Time Off Work:

Not every parental leave plan provides paid time off. As such, being off of work to welcome your bundle of joy may not be fully covered and paid. By understanding the parental leave benefits you are entitled to ahead of time, you can plan to navigate any loss of income before your child arrives and you have a newborn and all the responsibilities that go along with that.

Calculate Available Paid Leave: Determine the amount of paid leave you are entitled to. Calculate the income you will receive during your leave period to assess your financial needs and plan accordingly.

Explore Short-Term Disability Insurance: If available, investigate whether your employer offers short-term disability insurance. This coverage can provide a portion of your income during your leave period if you experience a medical condition related to pregnancy or childbirth. It is important to consider whether getting this insurance after becoming pregnant affects any benefits offered.

Build an Emergency Fund: This has been said in previous chapters but is a very important step. In the months leading up to your pregnancy or your baby's birth, strive to build an emergency fund to cover unexpected expenses or income gaps during your leave. Save a portion of your income each month leading up to your leave to ensure you have a financial cushion to rely on.

<u>Adjust Your Budget</u>: Be prepared to modify your budget to accommodate your reduced or eliminated income during your leave. Prioritize essential expenses, such as housing, utilities, food, and healthcare, and identify areas where you can cut back temporarily. Revisit the budget once you return from leave and your income stabilizes.

<u>Explore Government Programs and Benefits</u>: Research government programs or benefits available to new parents in your country or region. This may include childcare subsidies, tax credits, or assistance programs that can help alleviate the financial burden during your leave.

5.3 Possible Sources of Alternative Income During Leave:
In addition to trying to mitigate the loss of income through saving or cost cutting, you or your partner may consider looking into ways to make alternative income. This can be done in a variety of ways and can be tailored to your specific needs and family.Some possible avenues to consider are:

<u>Alternative work options</u>: Determine how much of your job requires you to be physically present in the office. If work-from-home is possible for your job or even parts of your job, inquire with your employer about the possibility of working remotely full or part-time.

<u>Paid Parental Leave</u>: Determine if your employer offers any paid parental leave benefits beyond the legally required minimum. Some companies provide extended paid leave to support employees during this important life event.

<u>Shared Parental Leave</u>: Some states and organizations also offer fathers and non-birthing parents leave. Determine if this is an option and look at shared parental leave options that may allow both parents to take time off work consecutively or concurrently. This arrangement can help manage the financial impact of a longer leave period. Additionally, it will allow both parents time to bond with their new baby.

<u>Side Hustles and Gig Economy</u>: Explore the gig economy and side hustle opportunities that can provide financial flexibility during your leave. This can include activities like tutoring online, ride-sharing services, freelancing, or selling products online. It may not make up for all your lost income, but it could lessen any financial impact. It helps if you prepare for this before your parental leave and your child's birth. A side hustle/gig should not be an extra source of stress, so it may be too overwhelming for new parents. If so, it's better to leave it be and adjust your spending habits instead.

<u>Utilize Savings and Investments</u>: If you have savings or investments, consider whether utilizing them during your leave is financially viable. Evaluate the potential impact on your long-term financial goals as well as tax implications. Use this information to assess the appropriateness of accessing these funds to support your family during this time.

Planning for maternity and paternity leave is a crucial aspect of financial preparation before starting a family. Understanding your rights and benefits, assessing your financial situation, and exploring alternative income sources can help ensure a smoother transition during this period. Be proactive in communicating with your employer, make necessary adjustments to your budget, and explore available resources and programs. By effectively planning and managing your finances during your leave, you can focus on caring for your newborn without unnecessary financial stress. Remember that every family's situation is unique, and it's important to evaluate and tailor your financial plan based on your specific circumstances.

6

Saving For Your Child's Future

As parents, one of the primary concerns is providing a secure future for your children. This chapter will explore various saving options and strategies to help you build a strong foundation for your child's future. This chapter provides basic information about college savings plans, other long-term savings options, and effective strategies for maximizing savings and compounding growth. For more in-depth information, consult a certified financial adviser to discuss and create a detailed savings plan.

6.1 Introduction to College Savings Plans:

There are many different ways to save for your child's education. As with everything else about having a kid, nothing is one size fits all. The important thing is to put some thought into the process and get started on saving. Remember, you can change your approach any time your finances change and many of these options are transferable between children if you plan to continue to grow your family.

1.<u>529 College Savings Plans</u>: A public 529 plan is a tax-advantaged savings plan to be used specifically for educational expenses. This includes state-sponsored college savings plans. It allows you to contribute funds that grow tax-free and can be withdrawn tax-free for qualified higher education expenses. Understand the types of 529 plans available, their investment options, and the contribution limits set by each state. These plans are fairly low maintenance and flexible; however, make sure you understand all fees associated with the plan. 529 plans can be started before you are pregnant, and you can name your child as a beneficiary later. Anyone can contribute to these accounts, so it makes a great way for grandparents, friends or other relatives to contribute to your child's future. Additionally, you can transfer the plan to a new beneficiary, tax-free, if that person is within the immediate family of the current beneficiary (sibling, step-sibling, parent, child, 1st cousin, niece/nephew), should your child not choose higher education. These plans can also cover eligible vocational and trade schools, K-12 education, off-campus housing and student loans. Removing money from the account for non-education purposes results in paying federal income tax on the withdrawal and a 10% penalty. If your child receives a full scholarship to college, the penalty for non-education withdrawal is usually waived. Each state has its own public 529 plan and most allow out-of-state residents to use their plans, so make sure to shop around.

2.<u>Coverdell Education Savings Accounts (ESAs)</u>: ESAs are another tax-advantaged savings option for education expenses. They offer more flexibility in terms of investment options, allowing you to invest in a wide range of assets. Contributions are not tax-deductible, but withdrawals for qualified education expenses are tax-free. ESAs cannot be opened for people over 18, and contributions are no longer allowed once the beneficiary reaches the age of 18. All assets within the account must be withdrawn by the time the beneficiary is 30. However, exceptions can be made for beneficiaries with special needs. Take note of the annual contribution cap. Currently, annual contribution caps are $2000. This amount is per individual beneficiary, meaning if they have two ESAs, they can still only have $2000 total contributed in a year (e.g., $1000 each account). Income and contribution caps apply, so make sure you understand before starting one of these accounts. ESA funds can be used for qualified trade and vocational school expenses but cannot be used for student loans. While seemingly not as flexible as a 529, ESAs are a popular choice for saving if you are concerned you will have additional K-12 education expenses. There is no annual limit on tax-free withdrawals for this type of expenses.

3.<u>Prepaid Tuition Plans</u>: Prepaid tuition plans are also available. These are also known as private 529 college savings plans, Qualified Tuition Programs (QTPs) or Prepaid Education Arrangements (PEAs). These plans allow you to pay for future college tuition at current rates. These plans offer the benefit of locking in tuition costs at today's prices, protecting you from future tuition increases. This usually means you are buying credits that are redeemed later. Think of it as paying for college hours now, but you won't be taking the classes until later. While prepaying tuition may sound ideal, this money may not grow like a typical 529 plan and it may not cover all expenses associated with higher education. For example, room and board may not be covered. Additionally, some of these plans have very narrow application windows and can be limited to in-state residents only. Be sure to research the availability and limitations of prepaid tuition plans in your state or region.

6.2 Other Long-Term Savings Options:

Education focused accounts are not the only option. Sometimes people get stuck on those because they state they are for educational purposes so we think there must be a specific benefit to them that is not offered by saving other ways. This is not always true. Money can be saved and grown in other accounts and still used for education. Also, you may prefer to give your child a financial cushion that doesn't require it being spent on education expenses. Some other options for saving for your child's future include:

Investment Accounts: Consider opening investment accounts dedicated to saving for your child's future. These accounts offer more flexibility in terms of investment choices and can be used for any purpose, including education expenses.

High-yield Savings Accounts: If you prefer not to risk your money by investing, you can search for savings accounts that give you a higher interest than may be common at most banks. Many of these accounts can be opened online in under 30 minutes and have no minimum deposit required. This makes them an attractive option if you are starting small or just need a place to set money aside that will still grow at a modest rate while you decide on a more specific education or investment account.

<u>Trusts:</u> Explore setting up a trust to manage and protect assets for your child's future. Trusts can provide control over how the funds are used and ensure that they are managed according to your wishes. You don't have to be rich to utilize or create a trust. Consult with an estate planning attorney to determine the most suitable trust structure for your needs.

<u>Custodial Accounts:</u> Custodial accounts, such as Uniform Transfers to Minors Act (UTMA) or Uniform Gifts to Minors Act (UGMA) accounts, allow you to hold and manage assets on behalf of your child until they reach the age of majority. This age varies by state but usually is between 18 and 21.These accounts provide flexibility in terms of investment options and can be used for various purposes, including education expenses. There are contribution caps on these accounts and taxes will apply to withdrawals. Please note that once the child reaches the age of majority, that money will be theirs to do with as they wish. Preparing your child to manage this money would be an essential step if you choose this type of account.

6.3 Strategies for Maximizing Savings and Compounding Growth:

Setting up an account for your child is the first step, there are other methods to help maximize the growth of these accounts. While being able to save more will always lead to a higher outcome down the road, even saving a little every month can have a positive impact on your child's future. Here are some strategies for maximizing this growth:

- <u>Start Early</u>: Time is a powerful ally when it comes to saving for your child's future. The earlier you start, the more time your savings have to grow, courtesy of compounding interest. If you save $50 a month for 18 years and put it in an investment, savings, or education account that gets a 3% annual return, that would be over $14,000. That is nearly $4,000 more than the $10,800 you would have if you shoved that $50 into a jar every month. However, if the jar is your preferred method, then put it there. $10,000 is better than nothing after all. Begin saving as soon as possible, even if it's with small contributions, and increase your savings over time.

- Set Specific Savings Goals: Determine how much you aim to save for your child's future education or other long-term goals. Set specific savings targets and create a plan to achieve them. Break down your goals into manageable milestones and track your progress regularly.

- Automate Savings: Automate your savings by setting up automatic transfers from your paycheck or bank account into your chosen savings or investment accounts. This ensures consistent contributions and removes the temptation to spend the money elsewhere.

- Take Advantage of Employer Benefits: Explore employer-sponsored benefits that can help you save for your child's future, such as matching contributions to retirement accounts or offering flexible spending accounts (FSAs) and HSAs that can be used for dependent health care expenses.

- <u>Regularly Review and Adjust</u>: Periodically review your savings strategy and adjust as needed. Consider increasing your contributions when you can, reassess your investment choices, and ensure that your savings plan aligns with any changing financial situation and goals. Set a yearly reminder on your phone to review your savings plans and check in on how well you are progressing towards your goals.

- <u>Involve Your Child in Saving</u>: Teach your child the importance of saving from an early age. Encourage them to contribute a portion of their own money toward their future goals. This instills financial responsibility and helps them understand the value of saving and compounding growth. It is important to teach your children how to manage their money to help them achieve their goals and learn patience.

Saving for your child's future requires careful planning, thoughtful consideration of various savings options, and disciplined strategies. College savings plans like 529 plans and ESAs offer tax advantages for educational expenses. In contrast, other long-term savings options, such as investment accounts and trusts, provide flexibility. By starting early, setting specific goals, automating savings, and regularly reviewing and adjusting your strategy, you can maximize savings and take advantage of compounding growth. Remember, each family's financial situation is unique, so tailor your savings plan to your specific needs and consult with a financial advisor to ensure you make the best decisions for your child's future.

7

Estate Planning and Wills

Although it may seem morbid, estate planning is a crucial step when starting a family. It involves making decisions about managing and distributing your assets and provisions for any minor children in the event of your incapacity or passing. This chapter will explore the importance of this process, the significance of naming guardians for your child, and the process of creating a will and establishing a trust if necessary. Remember, this is just an outline and not meant to substitute meeting with a certified financial planner and a qualified attorney.

7.1 The Importance of Estate Planning:

No one wants to think about anything bad happening to themselves or people they love. However, life is unexpected and as a new parent, you have a responsibility to your child to ensure that they are looked after at all times. You may think "I don't have much money, so it doesn't really matter" but it does. Estate planning is more than just money, it is also making sure your wishes for your self, in the case of incapacitation, and your children are respected while you can voice them. This can include the following:

Protecting Your Family's Future: Estate planning allows you to ensure your family's financial well-being and security in the event of unforeseen circumstances. No one likes to think about bad things happening but having a plan should the worst happen is an important safety net for your family. It helps protect your assets, provides for your loved ones, and minimizes potential conflicts and disputes during an emotional time.

Appointing Decision-Makers: Estate planning allows you to appoint trusted individuals to make financial and healthcare decisions on your behalf if you become incapacitated. This may be your spouse, sibling, parent or trusted friend. Additionally, these may be the people who you wish to have care of your child should anything happen to you. Having these conversations now ensures that your wishes are respected, people are comfortable and aware of their role, and that any important decisions are made in your and your child's best interest.

Minimizing Estate Taxes: Proper estate planning can help minimize estate taxes and ensure that more of your assets are preserved for the benefit of your family. Understanding tax laws and utilizing appropriate strategies can potentially reduce the tax burden on your estate.

Avoiding Probate: Estate planning can help your family avoid the often lengthy and costly probate process. By establishing a comprehensive plan, you can ensure a smoother transfer of assets and minimize administrative burdens for your loved ones.

Having a plan can save you and your loved ones a lot of trouble during a time where emotions would be high. Additionally, by having everything laid out before hand, it avoids any conflict or confusion which could make a situation worse.

7.2 Naming Guardians for Your Child:

This is a critical step for a new parent. There are many things to consider when looking into who you would like to be your child's guardian in an emergency. You may think you don't need to choose, people would just know, but if the parents die without a legal will in place, the courts will get involved in the placement of any children. This may result in the children being placed in foster care until a guardian can be named. A legally binding document can help smooth the transition and avoid that outcome. Taking this into account, it is important for parents to put time into the following:

- <u>Choosing a Guardian</u>: Naming a guardian is one of the most critical decisions you will make as a parent. Consider individuals who share your values, can provide a loving and supportive environment, and are willing to take on the responsibility of raising your child if something were to happen to you.

- <u>Open Communication</u>: Engage in open and honest communication with the potential guardians to ensure they are willing to accept the role. Discuss your expectations, values, and wishes for your child's upbringing to ensure alignment.

- <u>Documenting Your Choice</u>: Include your choice of guardian in your will or other legal documents. Be sure to review and update your selection periodically to account for any changes in circumstances, relationships, or the birth of additional children.

- <u>Temporary Guardianship</u>: Consider establishing temporary guardianship arrangements in case of short-term emergencies or situations where you may be temporarily unable to care for your child. These do not have to be with the same people you would have take custody if you passed away. Instead it could be family or friends who live near you and could allow the children to continue their normal routine for a short-time. Build in contingencies for if the short-term turns into a long-term situation.

Having people agree and know that you are naming them as possible guardians for your child will give you peace of mind. Again, this is something you can change at any point throughout your child's life as situations change. Make sure whoever you choose as a guardian knows where the will or legal document is located or what law firm to contact in case of an emergency.

7.3 Creating a Will and Establishing a Trust if Necessary:

Leaving your last wishes is a complex and emotional thing, but with the birth of your child, it is a very necessary thing. Work with your partner to make sure things are written down and allocated as you both desire. For the best outcome, it is important to:

- <u>Understand the Basics of a Will</u>: A will is a legal document that outlines how your assets will be distributed after your passing. It allows you to name beneficiaries, appoint an executor, and specify any other wishes you have regarding the management and distribution of your estate.

- <u>Consult with an Attorney</u>: Consult with an experienced estate planning attorney to help you create a comprehensive and legally sound will. They can guide you through the process, ensure your wishes are properly documented, and address any complex aspects of your estate.

- <u>Consider a Trust</u>: Depending on your circumstances, establishing a trust may be beneficial. A trust allows you to manage and distribute your assets according to your specific instructions, potentially avoiding probate and providing additional asset protection.

- <u>Seek Professional Advice</u>: Seek advice from a financial advisor and an estate planning attorney to determine what is necessary for your situation. They can help you understand the different options available and assist in structuring your plans to align with your goals.

- Update Your Estate Plan Regularly: Regularly review and update your estate plan as your circumstances change, such as the birth of additional children, changes in relationships, or significant financial changes. Set yourself a yearly reminder on your calendar to review this plan.

- Make Sure Someone Knows Where The Important Information Is: Keep your documents in a secure location. Make sure more than one person, especially the executor of the will, knows where a physical copy is kept or who to contact (attorney, etc) to get the most recent copy. Make sure you also have a list of all places where you have accounts (banking, investment, subscriptions, loans, etc) and any passwords that may be needed. Make sure someone you trust knows where this list is as it can save your executor quite the headache and ensure all of your finances are dealt with properly and not lost in the shuffle.

Estate planning and creating a will are essential steps to protect your family's future and ensure your wishes are carried out. By engaging in estate planning, you can protect your assets, appoint decision-makers, minimize taxes, and avoid probate. Naming guardians for your child allows you to select individuals who will provide a loving and nurturing environment in your absence. Creating a will and establishing a trust, if necessary, provide additional mechanisms for managing and distributing your assets according to your wishes. Seek professional advice to navigate the complexities of estate planning and ensure your plan is tailored to your specific needs. Remember, estate planning is an ongoing process, so regularly review and update your plan as circumstances change to provide ongoing protection for your loved ones.

8

Conclusions

Understanding and managing your finances is vital when start-ing a family. It enables you to create a solid foundation for your future and provides financial security for your loved ones. Having a handle on your finances can also reduce stress during a time that will likely be overwhelming.

Budgeting is the cornerstone of financial success. By creating a budget and tracking your expenses, you gain control over your money, allocate resources effectively, and make informed decisions about your spending habits. A well-crafted budget allows you to plan for the costs associated with having a baby and ensures that you can provide for your child's needs while maintaining financial stability.

Insurance and healthcare are critical considerations for your growing family. Understanding health insurance coverage for pregnancy and childbirth, exploring other insurance needs like life insurance and disability insurance, and planning for healthcare expenses are essential steps in safeguarding your family's well-being. Additionally, knowing your rights and benefits regarding parental leave allows you to plan financially for time off work, ensuring you can spend quality time with your newborn without jeopardizing your financial stability. Exploring alternative income sources during parental leave can provide additional support during this transitional period.

Saving for your child's future is a long-term commitment that requires strategic planning. College savings plans, such as 529 plans and education savings accounts, offer tax advantages and help you accumulate funds for your child's higher education. Other long-term savings options, such as investment accounts and trusts, provide flexibility and potential for growth. By starting early, maximizing savings, and utilizing compounding growth, you can build a strong financial foundation to support your child's future aspirations.

Estate planning and constructing a will ensure that your wishes are respected and your family is protected. Estate planning involves making decisions about asset distribution, appointing guardians for your child, and considering strategies to minimize estate taxes and avoid probate. Creating a will and, if necessary, establishing a trust provide mechanisms to manage and distribute your assets according to your specific instructions. These steps offer peace of mind, protect your loved ones, and ensure financial security for future generations.

In conclusion, understanding your finances and implementing effective financial planning strategies are essential for starting a family. By budgeting wisely, securing appropriate insurance coverage, exploring parental leave options, saving for your child's future, and engaging in estate planning, you lay a solid foundation for your family's financial well-being. Remember, each family's financial journey is unique, so adapt these principles to suit your specific needs and consult with financial professionals to make informed decisions. With a proactive and comprehensive approach to financial planning, you can create a stable and prosperous future for yourself and your growing family.

9

Resources

1.U.S. Securities and Exchange Commission. (n.d.). Introduction to 529 Plans. SEC.gov. https://www.sec.gov/about/reports-publications/investor-publications/introduction-529-plans

2.U.S. Department of Labor. (n.d.). Family and Medical Leave Act (FMLA). Wage and Hour Division. https://www.dol.gov/agencies/whd/fmla

3.U.S. Department of Health & Human Services. (n.d.). Health Savings Account (HSA). Healthcare.gov. https://www.healthcare.gov/glossary/health-savings-account-hsa/

4.NerdWallet. (2023, April 27). UTMA & UGMA: Understanding Uniform Transfers & Gifts to Minors. NerdWallet. https://www.nerdwallet.com/article/investing/utma-ugma

5.OpenAI. (n.d.). ChatGPT. https://www.openai.com/

www.ingramcontent.com/pod-product-compliance
Lightning Source LLC
Chambersburg PA
CBHW060214260726
48658CB00005BA/2033